Every Other Weekend

Terry Condon

authorHOUSE

1663 LIBERTY DRIVE, SUITE 200
BLOOMINGTON, INDIANA 47403
(800) 839-8640
WWW.AUTHORHOUSE.COM

© 2005 Terry Condon. All Rights Reserved.

No part of this book may be reproduced, stored in a retrieval system, or transmitted by any means without the written permission of the author.

First published by AuthorHouse 02/24/05

ISBN: 1-4208-3260-3 (sc)
ISBN: 1-4208-3261-1 (dj)

Printed in the United States of America
Bloomington, Indiana

This book is printed on acid-free paper.

Photographer: Terry Condon

"Tim Hortons is a registered trademark of The TDL Marks Corporation and is used under licence by The TDL Group Corp. Reprinted by permission of The TDL Group Corp."

"Casino Rama is a registered trademark. Reprinted by permission of Casino Rama."

*Dedicated to Greg and Alex,
the two reasons that I live today!*

"I would like to say thank you to my friends and fellow workers at Weyerhaeuser. Without their support and understanding, I would not be where I am today. The resources put forth for my concerns and guidance are invaluable and made me realize that a large company can make everyone feel important. All you have to do is ask."

Forward

The book you are about to read is written through my eyes. This is my perspective, and there are always two sides to every story. Read it and take from it what you need!

I would like to acknowledge some people, for if it wasn't for them, you would not be reading the following book.

<u>Cheryl</u> – the lady who not only saved my life but also made me realize that I did have something to live for!

<u>Donna</u> - the lady who gave me confidence to begin writing this book and the confidence to move on!

<u>John</u> - the man who along with his family, gave me a warm and secure place to stay, the desire to start reading, and an opportunity to express my inner feelings!

<u>Randy</u> -the man who was there for a game of golf and a good deal of friendly ribbing, the strong silent type!

<u>Niki</u>– the lady who started out as a great listener and became a long lasting friend!

And of, most importance,

<u>Towanda</u>- through all of this, she has made me realize that someone really loves Terry Condon for who he is!

Every Other Weekend

Every Other Weekend

Every Other Weekend

This is not a story about failure or the end, rather it is about how life can change in a minute, and with a strong heart we can learn to start again. "Every Other Weekend" is society's quick reply when asked to decide the fate of a father, his children, and their right to share life's most precious moments together.

Books, movies and songs all have a specific starting point, however this one does not. Oh, it probably does, but that is something I will never know. That moment is locked in the mind of my children's mother and it is something that will never be exposed to the world.

For reference I will use the cold November night in 2002. We were in the middle of building what was supposed to be our dream home in the small community of Wyevale, Ontario. A few days earlier I had mentioned that we needed to take a break from the stress of building a house and spend some quality time as a couple. She had a different opinion. It was that night when the coldest words ever to be used were echoed in the Condon household. "I don't love you anymore. I have felt this for over a year, but I didn't know how to tell you."

The day the shuttle exploded, the day the twin towers were attacked, the day they buried my mother – none of them compare when it comes to the pain, shock and devastation I felt that night. How could my wife of nearly 15 years suddenly stop loving me? We didn't fight, I didn't abuse her physically or mentally and I was a loving father of two great boys. How could she? I will never know. Instead I will fast forward to June 30th, 2003. That day we decided, or should I say, she decided that what we had was not worth fighting for. It was Canada Day 2003. The day at Little Lake Park in Midland was to be the last public appearance by the Condon's as a loving family. We laughed, we ran, we ate and then I said goodbye!

As soon as the boys were asleep in their beds, I begged my wife one last time to give us another chance, then backed down the driveway and drove off to start my new journey!

The first night of my new life was in the back of my dark blue Jetta TDI. Parked at the popular town dock of Midland, the hardest part of falling asleep was facing the fact that when you wake up, all the issues will still be there.

How do you explain to your children that you can't be there when they wake up looking for a hug in the middle of the night?

Why is it that there are so many people willing to help and care for you, yet the person who you lived with and loved for 18 years simply doesn't?

How do you wake up when you know what is about to unfold?

"You never look at others until you are in the same situation and then all of the sudden your heart opens up to listen and you learn from their hardships."

Every Other Weekend

Tim Horton's

Tim Horton's, the staple of my Saturday mornings.

A coffee chain so simple in design, yet it will provide both the highs and lows of all my weekends to come.

Coffee and Saturday mornings were never a part of my life, but since July 14th, 1998, they have been essential to my survival.

Greg and I started the ritual when he was only 4 days old. Coffee, bagel and a muffin was the usual order.

Everyone, especially an elderly lady that was there religiously like us, became fond of Greg and his sweet, innocent actions.

God, I wish for those days again.

Five years later and we still look forward to these mornings. Even more so since Alex arrived and he has had no problem fitting in. No time limit. Just drinks. Coffee for me; and for the boys it is a medium hot chocolate with a cup of ice cubes on the side to cool it off.

Together we watch the faces that come through the door, construction workers, families, and even some people that look like they are just coming down from a party from the night before. Maybe they were drowning their sorrows at the local drinking establishment.

Tim's supplies my required dose of reality as well.

There are those days when hockey is cancelled or the roads are too dangerous to travel, that I relinquish myself to that corner 4-seater and watch as life passes by.

It is because of this time that my ability to read individuals has become even greater. With each person that walks through the door, I try to comprehend what life they are living. Are they single? Have they lost a loved one? Do they have a promising future? Are they living the same hell as me? Or were they lucky enough to be surrounded by a loving family?

I have sat and looked out at the snow falling down in the parking lot, and wondered what it would be like to live someone else's life. Maybe people are looking at me and trying to guess my situation too.

All I know is that no matter how good or bad I have it, somebody will be worse off and somebody will always be better off. It is my life, and I will have to live it as best as I can. "Can I help you sir?" says the sweet voice of the young girl working the counter. "That will be a large regular to go, thank you."

Groceries

Could it be the hardest part of every other weekend? Just imagine, two boys under the age of six, filled up with hot chocolate and now in a wide open store full of running room. Did I mention the fact that there is nothing to keep their interest over the next thirty minutes? Oh there is one thing. There is the outside possibility of being able to pick out another two dollar Mattel Hot Wheels car. A cool one to add to the collection that already exceeds one hundred. This car is only available to little boys who listen the whole time we are inside Zehrs! Okay, for those who listen for the last fifteen minutes, okay the last five minutes and promise to be good in the car. This usually works because the list hardly changes; apples, bananas, bread, chicken, fruit roll-ups, milk, and of course, Cinnamon Toast Crunch cereal. It is our favorite. What better way to start a morning, than with a bowl full of sugar. We all know the routine for shopping, and the expected lack of focus occurs during the scanning of the day's purchases. Both Greg and Alex want equal duties when it comes to pushing buttons and placing items in the bags. Oh yes, I almost forgot about the washroom break. This process takes place when the grocery cart is at the furthest point from the washroom facilities. It creates sudden panic for all involved. I am sure the full cart at the bottom of the stairs draws the attention of fellow shoppers. Oh, how I wish that I had a spouse here like the other families we see. The proud part of grocery shopping is that in all this time, we haven't broken a single item. A small feat for three men in a food store with aisles of glass and towers of food items but at least it is a step in the right direction.

Every Other Weekend

Traffic

Heading home from work, and need to know the latest traffic conditions? No need to listen to the radio, just ask a single father when it is his day to be with his children. Traffic on these days, Tuesday, Thursday and every other Friday for me, can be described in one phrase. "Moving at a snail's place." How can it be that an 75 minute trek home all of a sudden becomes two hours on the days I need or should say *want* to be home sooner. Weather and road conditions follow a similar pattern. This past winter went like clockwork. Monday, Wednesday and alternate Fridays consisted of clear skies, no precipitation and dry pavement. My nights consisted of any or all of the following combinations: slippery roads, reduced visibility, and heavy snowfall. These are the perfect ingredients for creating road rage. I have been fortunate enough to know my limitations on fighting. Otherwise, face to face combat would have occurred many times. Make no mistake; the other drivers were not at fault. It was simply the fact that I wanted to be home with Greg and Alex and every other vehicle on the road was responsible for my tardiness. Kids, like adults cannot comprehend real time when they are expecting something or someone. Five minutes actually feels like twenty and being on time still feels like you are late. At two and five, the boys have not experienced the challenges of leaving the office on time, nor have they enjoyed the frustrations derived from commuter traffic. Seven years of driving 127 kilometers one way was never a problem, but now, with my loved ones waiting for me, even 12 kilometers is too far. Working from home seems like the only acceptable solution. Problem for me is that there is no home.

> **"The most important aspect of a promise is the ability to keep it!"**

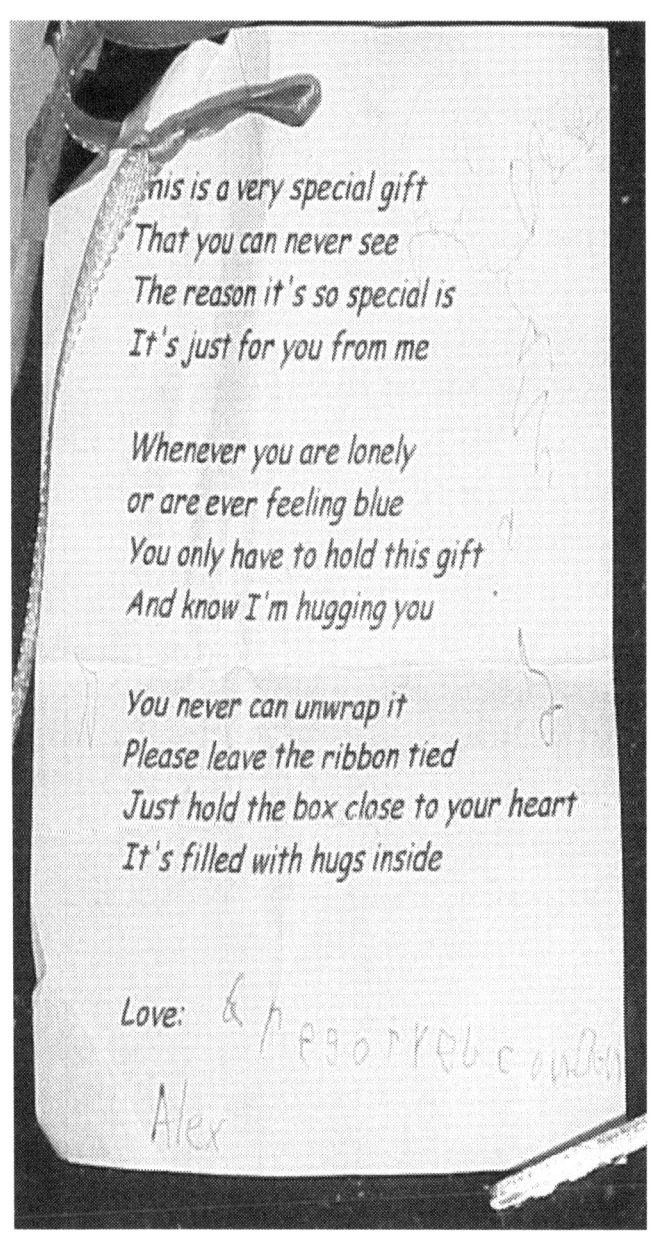

Suicide

Suicide: the coldest word in the English vocabulary. Haven't we all thought about it, to one degree or another?

Yes, I thought about it. In fact I seriously considered it at one point in this ordeal. Why didn't I follow through? At first I wasn't sure, but now I know that the main reasons are Greg and Alex. How could they ever talk about me to their children and be proud knowing that I gave up completely? It would be so much easier if I had. The pain wouldn't be there. No more sleepless nights. No more days of feeling lost. I hate all these bad times, but as Garth Brooks wrote in his song "I could have missed the pain, but I would have had to miss the dance". The pain of living is offset by the smiles and unconditional love given to me by my sons, and hopefully by even more individuals in my future. The future will be brighter for me and the boys. I believe this in my heart and because of all the people I have who support me. If I didn't believe this, then I wouldn't be alive today. Very few people in this world allow themselves to wake up knowing that all the future holds is more punishment. We, as a society, tend to look at the homeless, the ones begging for food as the weak ones. I don't. These people go to sleep in gutters and cardboard boxes every night, yet they wake up. Yes, they wake up knowing that the odds are they will once again endure the same hell as the day before. I think these people breathe because they believe that one day good luck will come their way. Many a person has stopped themselves from ever reaching this point. There are the jumpers, the wrist-slashers, and the pill takers. These are the obvious ones. What about the cunning ones? The car crashes. While evidence is minimal, I believe that some head on crashes are not accidents! At the beginning of this turmoil, the exact same thought crossed my mind. It was the perfect solution. The pain would end, the insurance would look after the kids, and because it would be considered an accident, nobody would think any less of me. It was perfect; all except for one thing. I couldn't begin to imagine not being there to watch Greg and Alex turn into teenagers, and parents themselves. I wasn't going to miss that. When it comes to people wanting to take their own lives, standard of living is not what dictates the ability of one's self to go on. Belief in a brighter future is the single most deciding factor. Greg and Alex are my deciding factor.

Halifax

July 30, 2003. It was suppose to be my 15th wedding anniversary. She had the house and I was about to sleep in my car. Not tonight I decided. Tonight, instead I was going to take a trip.

The trip I had to make. A trip to a place I had never been, and now I place I know I will never forget. I touched down at a small airport in the wee hours of the morning. A nice airport but it was much smaller than Toronto Pearson International. I had no room reservations, no idea where to go or how to get there. All the hotels by the airport were fully booked. I asked an older gentleman at the Hertz car rental agency about where he suggested I stay. "The Halifax Casino and Conference Centre!" was his reply. Perfect, I'll stay at a place of high rollers as I begin to gamble on the next stage in my life. It was a thirty minute bus ride at 1:00 in the morning. It was too dark to see the countryside; but dark enough to hide my fear and face from all the other passengers. I never fell asleep that night as I had to make a phone call in the morning and excitement kept my eyes wide open. Gambling on the $10.00 blackjack table kept my mind occupied. Six hours worth and I even managed to win. As the sun peeked over the horizon, I noticed where destiny had brought me, a beautiful ocean harbor. The boardwalks! The pier! The ocean! What better place to be when you plan to meet the person who could be the answer to all your questions. I made the call before 10:00am to let her know that I was in town. I waited for what seemed like days, to finally see her. I made sure the rose I purchased at the local market was as perfect as a flower could be. I am not sure why though? I knew it would have to be put in the garbage before she went back home to her family.

I have heard talk about time standing still, and now I know exactly what it mean. The moment I saw that red dress in the distance, I knew it was Dawn. My heart stopped; my breathing became shallow and everyone on that pier seemed to disappear. I watched her walk towards me, dark sunglasses covering any expression she might have. I think I know the moment she spotted me, because a smile started to form. This was a big moment in my life and I now knew that my gut had lead me to make the right decision. The plane ride; the bus ride; the sleepless night; all of it didn't matter anymore. I departed Halifax that day knowing two things, two very important things. Dawn was never going to end up being more than a true friend and the kiss was everything I wanted and thought it would be. Will I ever go back? Someday. And when I do I know that we will meet again, perhaps at that same bench on that same pier. At that time, she will still have her life and I will have mine, with my boys by my side.

Every Other Weekend

The Car

The galactic blue Volkswagen Jetta TDI!; five speed, air conditioning and warm winter package. Purchased new in June 2001. Now as I head into the spring of 2004, the cool blue car has hit 200,000 kms.

Greg says that daddy has the coolest car of any, and I have just made it cooler with the personalized plates: "GREGALEX".

This Volkswagen is crucial to my survival. On those weekends without the boys, I have hit the road to pass the time away. When money is tight, it is my resource for sleep. The commuting has been easier, especially with the CD player playing all the songs that relate to the life I am living. The dark blue color resembles the Toronto Maple Leafs, the color of my eyes, and the mood I have been feeling. It has provided me with warmth, security, and all of the comforts of Home Sweet Home!

Next time, late at night when you notice a lone car sitting in a parking lot, realize that someone could be settling down for a good night's sleep. Who says homeless means sleeping on the streets? The lucky ones have a car to go to with their sleeping bag. My car, as it turns out, has ended up to be the place where I get the soundest sleep. Hotels are too big and empty, and sleeping at friends or relatives doesn't work for me. While at their houses, I feel that I am intruding and it hurts even more to see what I am missing. Happy families together add salt to my open wound. The seats in the Jetta are surprisingly comfortable, and with the right combination of recline and height adjustment, I can fully extend my body into a pleasant sleeping position. Security is of the utmost importance, so my parking locations are carefully selected. Truck stops along highway 400 offer the most protection.

Every Other Weekend

Truckers have been both courteous and protective of me. The deep sleep tends to last for three hours at a time and seven hours total is considered a good night. Lucky for me, my workplace has shower facilities, so I can get to the office, shower and dress before the rest of my fellow associates arrive. They probably think I am just a dedicated employee, showing up to work so early. Boy, I long for those days to show up late. Well, darkness is closing in and the truckers are pulling up next to my Jetta.

Good Night!

Eight Minutes

Eight minutes.

That is the average duration of the phone calls to Greg and Alex on the nights I am not able to be with them. There is not a lot of substance to the call, yet it feels so short. It should not feel this way, because a proper father should not have to communicate only by phone to the ones he loves.

Alex is usually first, as he yells to answer the phone, same time every night I call. My ex-wife and I have been routinely calling between 6:30 and 7:00 pm on the nights we are away.

Oh sure, there are those underlying attempts to sabotage these precious moments. All of a sudden bath time is scheduled when Daddy is going to call. Bubbles and underwater boats take precedent over having a talk with Daddy. We can talk to him tomorrow. They don't lose. I do!

I can't forget the times when a game is being played or their favorite DVD has just begun. On these calls it is a quick "Hi dad, I love you, I miss you; Is it your turn to be home tomorrow night? Bye! Love you".

These upsetting calls are erased quickly by the nights when I have the full eight minutes.

Alex is so enthusiastic, yet he has little to say. "Daddy? Are you coming home tonight? Daddy, can we play hockey in the basement when we get home? Can I be the goalie? Daddy? Daddy? Love you. Night!"

Greg is more of the talker and so should he be; only five years old yet he has the presence of a twenty year old. We talk about his day at school. "What did you learn?"

For all that he endures; Greg proudly goes on with his life. He listens well at school and has become so independent, yet, at the same time; he socializes extremely well with his fellow classmates.

Did he bring home a new book to read with Daddy? Did he eat up all his supper? The answer to supper is "well kinda Dad". Greg isn't a big eater, but the good thing is that he loves his veggies and fruits. Pizza is his favorite supper item and for lunch it is that old time reliable…peanut butter and jam. Actually, just jam for school lunches, being it a nut free school and all. It is a chore getting the boys to eat dinner. It is amazing how a five year old can be completely full at 6:30pm, yet an hour later he is ready for all the bedtime snacks available.

We talk about what we will do the next time we are together, (usually the next evening) and then the customary yet very important "I miss you Daddy. I love you. Good Night!"

When I say the words "I love you" first, both boys are quick to respond "I love you too." I know the thoughts are the same, but the effect is so much greater when it comes from them first. Each time I call, I find that they are eager to share their feelings with me. In fact, Greg has become extremely good at noticing any changes in my voice. And, if sadness is in the air, Greg will question me.

There is rarely any communication with their mother on these calls, and all I can hear in the background is that cold voice; the one that use to say "I love you" to me for fifteen years, now utters quietly "Say goodbye and push the button." The most devastating noise known to a dad far away from loved ones, the dial tone!

Someday, when I have my own place, the boys will have a web cam and so will I. This is when they will be able to see how much I really miss them. Maybe for some unexplained reason, they will be with me by then. Probably not, but that is the end goal that keeps me going. Good Night boys. Daddy loves you very much!

The Song

Let's see.

Before the song, there was the book. "Love you Forever" by Robert Munsch. A light blue book; showcasing a young boy in the act of depositing a watch into the family commode. It is in every bookstore and although it was first published in 1986, it will always stand the test of time. An incredible book, that every new parent should own.

> "I'll love you forever,
> I'll like you for always,
> As long as I'm living
> My baby you will be.

These are great words to live by, and the book is a great reminder for every family about how deep love is and how it lasts but I needed something more to call my own with Greg and eventually Alex.

I started to sing to Greg when he was one, and by the time he was two, he knew the words. Alex is two and a half, and like his brother, knows the words.

I remember one week when I had to work in Windsor, three and a half hours away from home, and Alex was very sad that Daddy wasn't home. Greg got on the phone, and at the age of four said "Daddy, how about I sing sunshine to Alex so he feels like you are here." I cried. This boy is already a man, and cares so much about his brother. A simple bedtime song, was teaching me and the boys about love, communication, and the importance of never forgetting, or giving up. The song is used as a party song when the three of us sleep together; it is used as a comforting song when Greg knows I will be gone for days, and it is used as a sign of forgiveness. One such time was when Alex was really mad and not listening at bedtime. I had to be a parent, not a friend and Alex took exception. As I picked him up, Alex, with three little tears on his cheek, laid his head on my shoulder and in a soft voice pleaded his request "Daddy, can we sing sunshine?" All was forgiven.

No matter what happens in the years ahead, I know that this song will always keep us together. In the future, I know that Greg and Alex will pass this on to their own children.

I have no idea how I decided on this short tune, however the words will never be forgotten and Greg and Alex both know that they are my sunshine and will never be taken away.

When I am alone but thinking about the boys, the words provide me with the much needed solace needed to make it through the night:

Every Other Weekend

You are my sunshine,
My only sunshine,
You make me happy,
When skies are gray.
You'll never know dear,
How much I love you.
Please don't take,
My sunshine
Away!

You are my sunshine,
My only sunshine,
You make me happy,
When skies are gray.
You'll never know dear,
How much I love youuuuuu.
Please don't take,
My sunshine
Awaaaaaay!

The Ex-wife

This is probably, no, definitely the hardest chapter I will write. Years from now, when all is forgotten, or so say all the friends, therapists and fellow people from broken homes, I will still sit back and wonder how a person could change so much in such a short period of time.

I remember when my mom passed away. I was just about to turn 17 and lost the most important woman in my life. I remember the phone call that day, the race to the hospital, the days waiting for the coma to break. It never did. I remember walking into the hospital room, moments after she passed away. Her skin, her eyes, the coldness! Was this how I would always remember her? Nope. God has a way of providing us with the ability to block out these moments and instead remember all the good we had.

The peanut butter and jam sandwiches cut into perfect triangles, and served to my brothers and I as we watched television. The softness and security of her fur coat on those cold winter nights. I remember being carried out half asleep as we left the homes of my parents' friends. I remember the night in Havelock, when, during game seven of minor hockey play-offs, my Mom was too nervous to come watch her baby play net. Instead she sat in the car waiting for Dad and I to emerge with the good news. I remember her soft curly blonde hair, and the glasses that sat on her face. Glasses that fit like they were there since the beginning of time. This is what I remember the most.

Not the dark days, or not so readily.

Every Other Weekend

I remember if asked, the day that Mom and dad sat me down in the back kitchen of our family restaurant. They had just arrived back from Toronto from what was supposed to be a routine check up. She had cancer before, but it was suppose to be cleared up, gone, vanished, and destroyed by the chemotherapy. The doctors were wrong. That day they had given Audrey Condon three to nine months to live. This time they wouldn't be wrong.

Fast forward to 2003

My marriage has died. The woman who I fell in love with 18 years ago is gone. The blonde, petite, attractive small town girl is no longer. The young lady, who gave birth to our sons, is now trying to take them away. Do I remember the hurt she has thrown? Do I remember the pain caused as I envision her with another man, a man I know? Do I remember the vindictive side, the part that says "If I want to, I can make sure you see your boys every other weekend and that is all?" I hope not. I hope that this will pass along with the other dark days. She was everything I could want. She was beautiful, yet conservative; Strong yet flexible. She took a keen interest in everything I did and was always supportive. The passion and love I felt for her will never be matched. However, in order to move on in life, I must learn to love in a different way, with a different perspective. She was dedicated to her work, and loved her husband, kids and home. Now, it is a distant memory, only to be mentioned to the kids, as they grow older and ask about our relationship. They will only hear the good things, the happy moments, the moments that created our family. The pain and suffering will be between her and I and nobody else. A house is built of wood, while a home is made from love. Greg and Alex will know that for fourteen years I had a home. They are fourteen years that I will never regret. My wife and my mother are the two women that I loved so much; now both are gone. One is in heaven, and one just down the street. Gone, but never forgotten.

"Happiness sometimes slips into your life through a back door that you didn't realize was left open."

Every Other Weekend

Hockey

Hockey!

Canada's national pastime and for my sons and I, the glue that keeps us together. Every day that we are together, hockey plays an important role in our relationship. On weekends, Greg plays minor hockey; forward at first but now he has the passion required for being a goalie. Nighttime is Maple Leaf hockey, although their mom has tried to get them to like the Detroit Red Wings. Other times are spent together playing hockey in the basement or in the driveway. For the weekends that are not mine, hockey is the opportunity for me to see the boys, even if it is only just an hour. I remember watching Hockey Night in Canada one Saturday evening. They were retiring Patrick Roy's number in Colorado. He was arguably the best goalie of his era. During his speech, Patrick mentioned how he was so glad that his Mom and Dad along with the rest of his family were able to be there. I cried. What if this is Greg or Alex in the future? Who would be on the ice? Mom and stepfather? Would they be along-side Dad and step-mom? This is not what I would have pictured. I guess in the grand scheme of things, all that matters is that the boys enjoy whatever sport they choose. And if they do become successful, I will want to be there to watch. Greg knows, and Alex will too, that if we don't have fun, we don't play. Hockey, like life is not about winning, but rather it is about working as a team. Dad has now become the coach and Greg and Alex are playing the game of life. The trophy at the end of the game is made of love, respect and internal happiness. Let's hope that the coach can get us there.

Holy Mackinaw!

Every Hotel Room

Every hotel is the same. Four walls of cold; lifeless survival. Brampton, Barrie, Midland, Bolton, they are all the same. One bed, four pillows, two on the bed and two tucked away in the bottom drawer of the dresser. Only once have I found pillows with any resemblance of feathers or softness inside. The bathrooms are the same; bone in color and every wastebasket has the same clear bag inside. The televisions are small, the remotes are the same and when turned on, the same options appear. Movie channels, regular television, or Super Mario. Movies are $8.95 and the titles will never appear on your bill. This is under the assumption that the majority of clients will choose the Adult Only channels. Why do we assume the worst of people? The phone never rings, because no one knows your there. Sleep is light and I am always up before the wake up call. The wake up call! It is something I purposely do to have the false sense of someone being out there who is worried enough about me to make sure I get up. The showers are lukewarm, the pressure is light and the showerheads seem like they are set for people five feet tall and under. The nice thing about hotel rooms is that there is no need to wrap a towel around myself. No need to hang up the towels, just throw them in the tub. The beds don't need to be made and it is okay to leave the television on all night. There is no curfew, the plastic keys make little noise but the most important aspect of every hotel room is you can curl up under the blankets, and squeeze the pillows tight whenever you want. Nobody can see you cry. It will be different one day, for I know that when on a vacation, I will definitely choose a Bed & Breakfast over the fancy hotels. Well, maybe not: I guess as long as you have that someone special beside you, a hotel room could truly be a warm loving place to spend a night. By the way, three pillows laid length wise gives you the opportunity to feel like you are hugging someone.

Every Other Weekend

Dad

Michael Emmett Condon! Mutt! Crazy Legs! Scoobie.

All of the above make reference to my DAD. He is seventy-six now and more than ever he is an integral part of my life. He is the only biological grandfather that Greg and Alex will know. They know of Grandpa Jim, who passed away a year after Greg was born. Jim is now up high in the sky alongside Grandma Audrey (my mom), and together, the two of them protect the boys for always.

As a young boy, you always seem to be striving to be your own person. You tend to try to break free of the family mould. I did too. I wanted to be known as Terry and not as "Emmett's son. I wanted, or so I thought, to be completely different than the man who raised me and my brothers and sister. At the age of sixteen, my priorities were quite different than that of my parents. Church is not important, girls are. Family matters can wait, cruising the city streets can't. Saving and investing money are crucial, unless of course you need to buy beer, play arcade games, go to concerts or make your car look and sound cool. Back then, my father offered plenty of advice, and now, looking back, it was pretty sound advice. I wonder where I would be now, if I had listened. I remember two years ago, as I embarked on our house building project. My father said and I quote "Don't build too big of a house, 'cause you never know what will happen in life." I know he meant job wise, but nonetheless, he was right. There are many nights when I have Greg and Alex that I wonder if I can be the father they need. Can I show them enough patience? Can I separate the line between trying to be their friend and their father? If I fail, what will become of their futures? By the time I start the next day at work, my doubts are gone! At my workstation, there are two pictures of my father and I when we played the Ontario Family Golf Classic. Seeing the two of us together proves to me that when a man loves his children, he will overcome any and all obstacles to make sure they live the life they need and deserve. I am living proof. There is another picture, which shows Alex and Grandpa sitting in the front seat of Dad's car. When you look closely at it, you can see that Alex has the same features as my dad. How can it get any better? I can see that someday, my youngest son will possibly grow up to be just like my Dad. For me, that is the icing on the cake. It is always hard for boys and young men to tell their fathers that they love them, or even to say thank you for all the years. Last summer, while playing golf, I found the courage to do so, and the resulting warm feeling inside will last a lifetime. My Dad knows how proud I am to have him and to know him. The greatest compliment someone can give to me is to say "You are so much like your father."

"Cats in the cradle"; a song by the late Harry Chapin includes the following verse: "And as I hung up the phone, it occurred to me, my boy was just like me yeah, my boy was just like me." Someday, if I do things right, my sons will feel the same. Dad; thanks for walking a little slower, as I was able to follow in your footsteps.

Every Other Weekend

Every Other Weekend

Barns

Barns! Old barns! New barns!

They truly reflect how society has changed over the years. I have set out to photograph all the old barns still standing throughout Simcoe County. These photos will have a place in my home for years to come, for they provide a glimpse of how the sanctuary of marriage was and should be. Have you ever noticed that the old barns never fall down? Oh sure, they lose some boards or some of the roof, but they never fully succumb to what Mother Nature throws at them. The foundation made of natural stone, usually from the same general area, remains long after the rest of the building is gone. The construction technique was generally the same, no matter what countryside it was in. The building of a barn was always a community celebration and families from all around came to join in the celebrations. Rarely was a barn painted, they were left natural and today all of them carry that same shade of weathered gray. Very few windows to show what was inside yet you always noticed that the family name was prominently displayed on the outside. Old barns deserted on an old country-side road, breaking the horizon of abandoned fields. They remain a true sign of historic beauty, craftsmanship and most important: they are the splitting image of a successful marriage.

Our grandparents and their parents created the sanctuary of marriage just like a barn was built. Think about it. Think about how our grandparents lived? The marriage was a community celebration, with families from all around joining in. Their parents, our great grandparents, created the strong foundation of family through perseverance and solid core values.

We see this in the old family photo albums. The home was basic, without a lot of glitter or extras. The relationships and turmoil were kept inside the home and not compared to others around. Each family faced their own issues and worked them out within those four walls. The marriages of our ancestors stood the test of time, but now society, like new barns has created the illusion that everything must be new, improved and nothing like the past. We use advertising, make-up, clothes to create the appearance of something that we are not. New barns, like marriages don't seem to stand the test of time. They crumble at the onset of the weakest of storms. Instead of bending and compromise, they are brittle and break. New technology keeps coming out saying that things can be made better. In reality, all we have to do is go back to what we had. Forget about comparing with the next family, appreciate what you have and learn to build from the ground up. Building out will only cause weakness. Someday, there will no longer be these old gray buildings darting the countryside. No reddish gray tin roofs, no colored stone foundations. All we will be left with are lifeless, personality free bland buildings. We will long for the old farms and long term relationships from days gone by. Love, like water and bread is what we need for society to grow and succeed. We need more old couples walking hand in hand. Remember this the next time you take a drive and notice the old gray barn standing alone in the wind!

Nine PM

This is bedtime for Greg and Alex. Actually, bedtime is eight o'clock, but by the time we brush our teeth, read a book, sing the song, and tickle some backs, it is now nine p.m. I remember how great this time was. Now would be the time that my wife and I would sit down, unwind, and communicate. I don't have that anymore. I have the noise of a television and the occasional sound of the furnace kicking in. No "How was your day?" No "Would you like to do something special this weekend?" There is very little noise when you are sitting alone. At times I want to go upstairs and tell the boys we can watch Treehouse T.V. until they fall asleep in my arms. One Saturday night, we brought down the blankets and pillows and set up shop for the night in the living room . Extra pillows were laid on the floor. Strategically placed, so when a youngster inadvertently rolled the wrong way off the couch; he had a soft landing. We watched the Toronto Maple Leafs play the early game, but before the puck dropped for game two, Greg and Alex were already in dreamland. It was the same quiet, but somehow, with the boys lying beside me, it just didn't feel as lonely. There is plenty to do after the kids are in bed, and I know that I was always prepared for some work as soon as the bedroom lights went out. All of the lights, except for the small red Santa Claus night-light that is used year round. Running to the store, or to Tim's is not an option, since there is nobody to keep an eye on the boys. No chance of going out on a late evening munchie run. That is replaced by eating ice cream or having a couple of peanut butter and jam sandwiches. Lots of peanut butter in the house, ever since Greg started asking for "just jam" sandwiches. I pass the time away by checking e-mails, looking at the Creative Memory albums and listening to music. The silence was broken occasionally by Alex calling to let me know it was time to go pee. This was true the first call, but as for the second and third calls, it was his way of being able to stay awake a little while longer. Great for him, tiring for me, but Alex is now sleeping through the night, moisture-free! Good news, it seems, turns out to be a negative for me. Remember the phrase "Careful what you ask for?" Believe it. I do. I am living it everyday now.

Want

The orange ball sets in the horizon. Half of the sun has disappeared, but the other half reflects across the calm seas of the South Pacific. In a short while, you will drift off to sleep as the waves lap against your private shoreline. Come morning, there will be fresh cut flowers, picked from your botanical gardens, arranged in a beautiful Ming vase, sitting upon a sparkling white breakfast table. The table is located on an open patio just through the terrace doors that open into a breathtaking study. The sounds of Van Morrison softly escape from the den, as you sip on a cold glass of fresh papaya juice.

Does this sound like everything you want? Not everyone has this lifestyle nor is it likely we will obtain it, yet for those of us who don't, we are quite content with our present situation and lifestyle. The reason is so simple; the majority of society believes, and lives the following theory; "It is not important to get what you want, but rather, you must want what you have. Kids are the perfect example of how this practice works. Every boy and girl, when walking through Toys R Us, wants all the toys, the new bikes, and the biggest play-sets. They may cry, and may even throw a fit if it is not in their possession upon leaving the store. The car ride home will most likely be hell, but when they get home, everything changes. Our children will carefully take stock of what toys they possess and within minutes, they have the uncanny ability to turn that old Buzz Lightyear action figure, or the broken dump truck into the ultimate play item. They are happy; they are content; and all because of one thought… .."This toy is all I have, so I better make the most of it. Kids learn at very young age, that in order to be happy they must "want what they got!

Every Other Weekend

Adults don't. So many of us look at what others have and than compare that to what we have at home. We want what others appear to have. Their fancy cars: the newest wardrobe: their exciting careers. Why? We built a home, a lifestyle, and now we want to change all that. The attractive middle aged blonde driving around in her BMW convertible, and wearing the latest in designer fashion. You want to be her? Actually, she is a widow who lost her husband and children in a horrific car crash two years ago. Everything she has is a result of the insurance policy and driving around is the only way she can cope with life. The big executive: wearing tailored suits and traveling around the world; experiencing unique cultures and exquisite cuisine. Staying in penthouse suites; financed by corporate America. Is this who you want to be? He has no family; no home and each of those nights spent in the suites are spent alone. No one to call at home! No one to buy souvenirs for! It is so important that we realize that others would love to have what we already have. Stop trying to always get what you want! Become a two year old and make the most of what you have. The smiles will come naturally.

"People often live their problems, not their possibilities"

Friends

When I was in public school, spelling the word friend was always difficult. The "e" and the "i" always got reversed. Finally, one day my teacher, Miss Gainey, sister of the now legendary NHL player Bob Gainey, taught me the spelling secret. Friends will stay together until the end. Remember this and your spelling will never go wrong. I believe I was seven or eight at the time, but it is not until thirty years later that I have finally come to fully understand her statement. Life for me can go on without my wife, but without friends, it would come to a screeching halt. Donna, John, Cheryl, Niki, Steve, Milena, Andy, Dave, Tanya, Randy, Clive and Jaimie. These are just some of the people that have made the path to the future a lot easier to travel. Each one has helped in their own special way; a patient ear, motivating speech, a place to lay my head down, or even a simple smile and "Good Morning". Each and every one of us has our own misfortunes in life, but it takes someone special to set those aside and focus on someone else. Honestly, I don't believe I have that ability. In my mind right now, the world is suppose to be waiting for me. I am truly sorry for this and hopefully the future will create a better me. How do you say thank you for all that your friends have done? Money means nothing, and in fact, it might be considered an insult. Gifts are not required, and public acknowledgment is waived. The more I contemplate, the clearer it becomes. All that my friends want is for me to heal and move on in my life. My ability to put the past behind will, in the end, say thank you to everyone who has stretched out a hand. Friends to the end. Friends: the ones who allow you to begin again. To all of you……. Thank you!

Music

The power of a song! The power of words! The telling of a story! The importance of song!

Music has been a source of therapy and relaxation throughout this process. Songs are a way for individuals to tell their stories to the rest of the world. Love songs, sad songs, songs of hurt and songs of celebration. There are stories of triumph, and courage. Stories of moving on, and stories of losing it all. No matter what the generation, society has had the same story to tell, just to a different beat. From Country & Western to modern day Jazz, every musician has been able to put to musics, all the feelings that I am becoming exposed to. Bob Seger, March Cohn, Natalie Cole, Norah Jones, Kid Rock, Cheryl Crow, Bryan Adams, Uncle Cracker'; all of these artists have been able to show me the way. Music tells the story, the turmoil that many of us, many more than we are aware of, have lived. Music is everywhere; in our car, in our house, at our place of employment. Everywhere we turn, there is music. There are the ones who are always humming a tune, and if you notice, these tunes are always ones of happy songs. Phil Collins along with Walt Disney has recently released a soundtrack from the children's movie called *"Brother Bear"*. This song is now my roadmap and the first verse goes like this;

"Tell everybody I'm on my way, new friends and new places to see. With blue skies ahead, yes I'm on my way and there's no where else that I'd rather be."

Here's to the special song in everyone's heart. Maybe we should all focus on trying to hum a happy tune! Remember the old Coke commercial?

"I'd like to teach the world to sing in perfect harmony"

Every Other Weekend

Counseling

I don't need counseling. I am not crazy. I am not paranoid. I know how I feel. I am not wrong. These are all the answers that I and many others use as an excuse to avoid the "couch". Just the mention of the word and many of us feel as though we have given up or have lost. I am now thankful. Thankful to those who persisted in making me set up that first appointment. It took me four different counselors before I found Barbara. She is the one that seemed to know what it would take to help me move on. I still remember that first visit. After waiting in the lobby of an old restored home, I was lead down some halls, up a old flight of stairs and then through a short maze of rooms before we came to my chair. My first impression was that she was somewhat sincere in her concerns for my future well being. That, in itself amazes me. For after all the lectures and previous cases, my story would probably pale in comparison. Barbara, simply in her silence, showed me that I mattered. She didn't question my personality traits, nor did she try to analyze why I was in this situation. All she wanted me to do was to be aware of my feelings and allow myself to set my own roadmap to the future. Her eyes alone, gave me a sense of self worth. And the open ended questions forced me to deal with my emotions. "If you didn't have a level head on your shoulders, I would be worried about you" she said. That statement will remain in my mind for the rest of my days. To me, it meant that I had a grasp on reality and with the proper tools, I could make it. I am very glad that I didn't stop after my first counselor and I have even suggested that one of my friends use the expertise of a counselor. They too, are doing much better. These people are professionals, and they genuinely care about our well being. Society is changing daily and not everyone is capable of keeping up with lifestyle changes. Use a counselor no matter how small you think your problem may be. It works, and in the end I now realize, "I am not crazy, paranoid or wrong. I have feelings and it is okay to feel these emotions as long as I understand why!

The First Date

Do you remember your first date as a youngster? Guys usually don't, but I know this first date of my new life and it will never be forgotten. Before I had even contemplated ideas of dating, a friend set me up on a blind date. It was with a younger woman from a small town, and because I have no idea how our futures will fall, she will remain nameless. She knows who she is and how special it was. I was so nervous during the one hour drive to pick her up. How did I look? What will we talk about? Will I compare her to my ex? Will we kiss? Do I tell her about my past? My kids? What if she doesn't like me? What if it gets serious the first night? Should I sleep over? Will I be able to perform or will nervousness take over? Do I have too much cologne on? Do I not have enough? Do I make the first advance or let her? Sound like a teenager? Well, that is exactly what I felt like. At one point I was ready to turn the car around and chicken out. Just, like everything else, I decided to take a chance and see what happened. It turned out to be the right choice. The initial greeting was one of apprehension on both parts, but we quickly became comfortable with each other. I must admit, for a first date, she was the right person. Dinner consisted of finger foods at a local restaurant and small talk quickly turned into real questions, and real conversation. It felt great to look into someone eyes and see that they were in tune with what I was saying and showed a keen interest. A glass of white wine and the superb cheesecake finished the dinner off on the right note. We laughed and listened to music on the way back to drop her off. I had, at this point, no intentions of going any further. Waking up in her arms the next morning was not in my realm of thinking. This would change quickly. The offer to come inside was gladly accepted and to sit on the couch together was something that I had greatly missed. The rubbing of the shoulders progressed to the tickling of the back and was followed shortly thereafter with small kisses. Small kisses turned into long kisses and intrigue turned into passion. Passion, not lust, is what I felt. The night became everything I could have imagined, but the morning was the highlight of the whole date. It had been over twelve months since I had the moment that I thought would never be taken away. I woke up in someone arms, kissed them good morning, and felt wanted. I felt warm inside and I had a great feeling about the day ahead. Romance, I guess is like riding a bike. If you fall and get hurt, it is a must that you get back up and try again. If you don't, there is that possibility that you become too afraid to ever try again. This new relationship and friend might very well turn into my next and hopefully last marriage. It might end after a month. I don't care. It is, and will be, a special moment of my life that will never be forgotten. This lady or should I say, young woman gave me the opportunity to have feelings again. She gave me the ability to express my emotions and she took all of me at face value. She appreciated our time together, and more importantly she was comfortable enough to say so. I thank you for teaching me how to get up and start life again, my training wheels are off and I am not scared of falling again. There is air in my tires and my handlebars are pointed in the right direction. I am going to enjoy the feeling of the wind in my face, as I head down this highway called my future, and you my dear will always be a part of what got me here. Thank you.

"The Price for forgiveness is to be able to forgive!"

Every Other Weekend

Goalies

Cement heads. Puck stoppers, Ghoolers, Puck Bag, Sieve. You have to be crazy to be a goalie. That is what people tell me. Crazy isn't the main ingredient; courage, self esteem and a desire to succeed are the characteristics of any competent goalie. That is why Greg and Alex are well on their way to becoming the next Patrick Roy. Actually, that's not true, for I told Greg that one day people might want to be like him, rather than he tries to be like someone else. *He* could be the standard that everyone strives for. He doesn't have to make it to the NHL; heck if all he plays is street hockey, that is okay as long as he has fun and does the best he can. It is far more important to know that you have done your best as an individual, than it is to come home with a trophy. Every goalie has experienced that game where you have played your heart out, only to lose in overtime by a shot deflected off of a defenseman's leg. Playing your heart out is more rewarding than sitting in the crease for a whole game as your team dominates the opposition. Greg, already in his early playing years, has experienced the thrill of adrenalin flowing through his body. He loves it and can't get enough. Alex so far, has only felt this while playing in the driveway or in the basement, but he too has a love for the position. Being a goalie is unique. You get to stand back and watch everything unfold in front of you. You learn to anticipate and to appreciate what others are doing in front of you as part of the team. You are able to watch two teams battle to obtain the all important win. For whatever reason, goalies put the weight of the world on their own shoulders, and in their own mind, bare full blame when a goal is scored. Goalies are always open to criticism from teammates, yet when offering an opinion, fellow teammates turn a deaf ear. Goalies are teased and ridiculed, but in the end, when answering truthfully, everyone will tell you that a goalie is the most important person on a team. The goalie, in fact, is usually the deciding factor when the big game is on the line. The goalie, in order to be successful, must be able to realize that while the game might have been lost, he has done the best he could. Losses early in his career will only contribute to his success later in life. I, as a goalie in the game of life, am involved in the toughest game in my career to date. Hopefully, all of this will make me a better goalie and person when the next challenge is put forth. My family, friends, and co-workers are the team in front of me and I know that when it comes down to the final minute, they will all hustle back to support me.

Venting

A book about this stage in my life would not be complete without a little venting, a little anger and a little confusion. Why does this have to happen? Why do people have to change? Why is the last 15 years of my life reduced to 25 pages of legal jargon? I am now able to understand all the new terms related to my future. They include: cougars, bar flies, available, in the game, Divorce Act, Ontario child support tables, irreconcilable differences and of course my favorite.....joint or shared custody. Remember the little kid in primary school that always ran to the teacher when things didn't go as planned, or someone picked on them? This, it seems, is the way society as a whole, has decided to deal with everyday life. If it is not perfect, let's start all over again. Second and third time marriages are more of a rule than an exception. I know of marriages where spouses are worse than I could ever imagine, yet they are still together. Why couldn't I have been given a warning or even a second chance? What annoys me most is when people, family and friends both, say to me "Oh yeah, we could see this coming", or "Yes, we knew she was really like that", or even better "Don't worry, you will be better off without her". Why didn't somebody say this before it happened? I hate the fact, that as I near the age of forty, I have to look at starting over again, and start the whole process of falling in love. It sucks. Bars are not a place I want to be, and checking out websites looking at women's "alleged" bios is even worse. "I yearn for a long walk on moonlit nights" has got to be the most used line on dating websites. Actually it is the second. The most used is, get ready for this: "I am looking for someone to make me feel complete." The statement should read; "I want to have fun and be loved, but I have been burned before so don't expect me to wear my heart on my sleeve. What you see is what you get." Push up bras, water filled bras, hair extensions, padded underwear, and control-top pantyhose. Why? Eventually the person you meet is going to see you naked. Why not be the person you really are? Why do people try to be something they are not? I know that it is just an opinion, but why the hell must we always look for negatives in people and situations. How do you deal with the idea of your children spending time at the home of your ex's lover? What do you say when your son asks "How come Mommy has a friend and you don't Daddy?" It's so frustrating when you look around for answers and there are none to be found. It's a Monday night and I am at the docks in my town of Midland. There are kids playing; older couples are sitting on the bench watching the boats pull into the harbor. This is a picture right out of Mayberry. I can hear thunder faintly in the distance, and soon a storm will be upon us. The town docks will soon be abandoned. I know it has to rain, but why tonight? Why now? I am not ready to be alone yet. It is too early in the evening. Oh, no, here comes the first drop. Rain is like a spouse's wandering heart. It's happening, and it is happening right now. I can't stop it. Instead, I have to try and look for the rainbow that will come after it is over. Damn this rain. Damn this life.

One Year Later

July 1st, 2004. 12:05am and I am sitting at seat ten on the $2/$5 poker table at Casino Rama. I have decided that instead of sleeping in the car or a hotel room tonight, I will pass the time away gambling with the other all-nighters. Everything we do in life is a gamble so why should tonight be any different? As it turns out, the $200.00 that I came here with will be down to $150.00 when I leave at 4:30am. Not a huge loss and I had all the free water and coffee that my kidneys could handle. The agreement was that I would have the boys starting at noon on Canada Day. This way the boys are able to spend some time with Mom and Dad on Alex's third birthday. There are big Canada day celebrations being held in our small town, and my ex is taking the boys there first thing in the morning. The house will be available around 8:30am, so I will find a dark corner at a carpool lot and catch a few winks until then. I got home, showered, and had breakfast by the time Greg and Alex showed up at 12:30pm. Rain had hit our town early in the morning so the boys did not get a chance to enjoy all the rides at the park. They did however, get a chance to have their faces painted, and have a breakfast birthday celebration with my ex's new boyfriend. As it turns out, when the boys got home, they hadn't eaten lunch. There was no desire to eat, as it was time for Alex to open his birthday presents. A cool skateboard won decidedly over the remote control four-wheeler, and we had been wise to get Greg the same skateboard. This prevented the feeling of being shorted in the eyes of a five year old. We played for about an hour and then it was time to head out for the go kart track and mini putt. In the time it took me to go upstairs and find shorts for the boys to wear, Greg and Alex had fallen fast asleep on the couch. A late evening combined with an early morning departure to the park produced two very tired boys. The next two hours of my time with the boys was spent sleeping on the couch. Oh well, I least I had them in my arms. After nap time it was a rush to get go-karts, mini-putt, and dinner in before bed time. We actually stopped on the way home to watch a local fastball game. The boys had never seen one, and when I heard "Daddy, can we please turn around so we can watch the game" come from the backseat, it was a no-brainer. It is Canada Day; it is Alex's birthday; the boys should be able to do whatever their hearts desire. That train of thought is exactly why I stopped at the playground and let them enjoy the swings too. It is weird that with all the toys they have, Greg, Alex and I laugh the most when playing on the swings. The thrill of flying higher and higher and having Daddy as the engine creates plenty of uninhibited laughter. It was now 8:30pm and we had to hurry home to get pajamas on, have a bedtime snack, brush our teeth, read a book and fall asleep. Freshly sliced watermelon, refrigerated and cold to the lips was the perfect end to our day. The chosen book was "Franklin Plays Hockey", and like other books we had a lesson learned by the end of the story. It was brought to Greg's attention that when he starts hockey this winter, there will be new kids on his team who are playing for the first time. It is okay if they don't play very well, and he shouldn't get disappointed if they lose some games. "Just like Franklin did for Skunk? Is that what you mean Dad?" Affirmation that the young boy lying beside me was indeed paying attention. Lights out, some back tickling, and the day is over. A year has passed, and so much has changed! My marriage, my friends, my social life, my outlook on the future and my sleeping arrangements for Canada Day have all changed. The only thing to remain constant in the past 365 days is that Alex and Greg are waking up in the night only to find one parent at home. Tonight it is me. I am gainfully employed, I have two great kids, I am separated, my wife is destroying me, and I am going to be paying support for the next twenty years while she will be well off. I am without a home of my own. In other words, like the beer commercial proclaims…"I am Canadian." Happy Canada Day everyone!

The Search

Okay, so the healing time is over. I have already encountered the hate stage, the disbelief stage and now it is time to start a new life with someone special. Where do I begin to look? The bar scene; The internet; blind dates? People have even suggested the grocery store or shopping malls on a Saturday morning. Twenty years ago when my dad had to start dating again, all he had were church groups and friends of friends. I tried the "friends of friends and I learned very quickly that the phrase "she has a great personality" has stood the test of time. The bar scene is scary these days. The young men are so loaded with testosterone that they want to fight at the slightest look that offends them. The girls; with their make-up, their clothes and their attitude makes a twenty three year old look like she's thirty The bars are packed with people who spend hours to become someone other than themselves. It's amazing how short skirts, revealing tops and lip gloss can take the caring and honesty out of a woman. The Internet! Now, isn't that a treat. There is Ashley Madison.com, Singles.ca, and my home....Lavalife.ca. Some of the seeking females are genuine and sincere, like the widowed lawyer I chatted with. I assume she must have orchestrated a credit check on me and decided that my bank account was not sufficient enough to provide for her future happiness. I am starting to understand the chat lingo, short forms such as L.O.L. (laugh out loud); S.W.F. and my favorite, B.B.W. There are the single females looking for true companionship and of course there are the attached females seeking intimate discreet encounters. Discreet encounters, yet they have their photos pasted across the internet. An oxymoron if I've ever heard one. Any time I have met someone through these internet services, I have been very confused and frustrated. They chat with you about anything and everything, yet give them your phone number and they never call. I have suggested meeting for a coffee or the idea of even going window shopping at a mall. The reply is that they are not sure until they know the person. It's kind of like the chicken and the egg; you are not going to know someone until you meet and talk face to face. I can only imagine what the men do in order to make themselves look appealing to women as well. Guys must be a pain to deal with when women are looking for a companion. I think, overall, I am just not interested in searching for a companion. Thirty nine years old, two kids, paying support to an ex and not having a home of my own, all contribute to making this more like work. Love is supposed to come naturally; however, right now I feel the only way to meet someone is to draw up a mate searching resume. Hmmmmm ! Should I list my ex as a character reference? Should I provide full financial disclosure? Is being with only four women in your life considered an asset or a liability? Should I include a cover letter outlining my intentions? Won't I look cute standing outside a Sobey's handing out resumes? Hey, it just might work. What have I got to lose?

Nothing……………………………..nothing at all!

<u>Wasted</u>

It's 10:30 am on Saturday morning. I would stay in bed, but my body says it has had enough shut-eye. The boys are away with their mom this weekend, probably on "his" boat on Georgian Bay. For the third time in the last year, I have the house to myself. I just finished eating my bowl of Cinnamon Toast Crunch and now it is time to decide how to fill the day. The neighborhood is quiet, except for the music echoing through my house. Martina McBride's "Where Would You Be?" just came on. Well, I am right where I want to be. Sitting on the front porch on a Saturday morning listening to the music; having a coffee with my wife and watching the kids play on our beautiful front lawn. Wait! Something is missing! Something is wrong! No wife beside me. No kids playing or saying "Watch this Daddy". The yard is empty, the street is empty and the house is empty. This is not where I want to be, But where do I go? Randy, the guy who loves to golf as much as me, has decided that today is the one Saturday all year that he will take a break from the game. Ron, my support buddy has his daughters this weekend and is heading to Kilbear Provincial Park. There is a big beach party happening in Port Stanley this weekend, but it is a four hour drive. I would only know two people, one of whom I tried a blind date with, and as we say in the office, "I am out of the loop" with the rest of the party crowd. John and Bridgette are in the Niagara area with Jeffery, and Steve and Cathy are busy with their girls. I think I will just ride my bike into town to kill some time. Lunch at Scully's and the ride back should kill about four hours of the day. An afternoon nap on the back deck, and then I can head over to the driving range and try to find my long lost golf swing. Home, shower, some dinner and then hit the couch for the rest of the night. Sarah McLachlan's "Arms of Angel" just came on. What a song for me to listen to right now.

> *Spend all your time waiting for that second chance*
> *For the break that will make it ok*
> *There's always some reason to fell "not good enough"*
> *And it's hard at the end of the day*
> *I need some distraction, oh beautiful release*
> *Memories seep from my veins*
> *They may be empty and weightless, and maybe*
> *I'll find some peace tonight*

The song is me. This beautiful day – wasted. This beautiful house – wasted. A day without the kids – wasted. The big green plush front lawn – wasted. The past year of my life – wasted. A good friend told me that I have to stop wanting it so bad. I have to wait and let love come to me. The companionship, the desire, the want, it will all come, but I have to wait. Is she right? Should I try this? Will I ever feel alive and loved again? Well……unsinkable ships sink, unbreakable walls break, you should never underestimate the impossible!

I guess lying in bed all day and keeping my eyes closed is the only way today could be a waste.

That won't happen…..at least not today!

Every Other Weekend

The Ring

"Diamonds are forever"

"Nothing says love like a diamond"

"Diamonds are a girl's best friend"

"Three months salary is a small price to say I love you"

All of the above are slogans used by diamond manufacturers and jewelry stores. We all buy into it, some of us more than others and it is evident by the size of today's diamond engagement and wedding rings. Makes sense doesn't it; a multi-millionaire must be more in love than a factory worker? If you can only spend $500.00 on a diamond ring, then your love mustn't be as deep as a man who has $10,000.00 to spare? A couple farming in the Midwest can't possibly feel the same degree of love as the jet setting couple from the city.

I remember when I first saw my wedding ring, I loved it. Rather than just a plain band, mine was set with small diamonds and to me it looked like a million dollars. I remember all the compliments received over the years. It meant something to me because of the love behind it. Well, beauty is in the eye of the beholder, and when the love is gone, a wedding ring has absolutely no value. I dropped into the local jeweler to find out what the ring was worth, and if there was something else he could make with it. "Twenty dollars Mr. Condon, I can give you twenty dollars for this ring or if you want, I can melt it down and create a small money clip."

Every Other Weekend

The money clip was out of the question, since any money I have will soon be in her possession. Twenty dollars was an insult, in fact I ended up suggesting that he only give me fifteen dollars. One dollar for each year of married bliss, and at least that put the value into perspective. Seems a waste to throw it into the garbage and I can't wear it, since I am no longer married and in love. Women, on the other hand never have this problem. All they do is wear the rings on a different finger. To them, the meaning of the ring doesn't matter as long as it looks good and is stylish. Wedding rings can actually be used in a dating situation, because for some reason, some women are attracted to you if you wear a ring. I guess the thought of screwing up someone else's life is a turn on. Friends have suggested that I get rid of the ring, but to do it in a ceremonial way. Throw it into Georgian Bay, or maybe out of the car along the highway. Bury it, or maybe even better, take it back to the restaurant where I proposed many years ago. They could put it through the garbage disposal, and therefore the ring could be like a piece of rotten meat, similar to how my ex feels about me. Maybe we should change our ways about the diamond giving process. How about if there is no ring given for an engagement, but the longer you are married, the bigger the diamond you receive. Make the ring a parting gift, as a token of appreciation for all the years spent together. A marriage of five years or less equates to a cubic zirconium and for every year after five your diamond increases in size by a quarter carat. This would mean that after fifteen years of marriage, a woman can walk away with a 2.5 carat diamond ring. This would replace any financial settlement. I have a feeling that separations would decrease dramatically when there is no financial incentive. Love should be determined by the amount of passion and commitment, not by the size of the diamond.

> **"Happiness lies for those who hurt, those who have searched, and those who tried, for only they can appreciate the importance of people who have touched their lives"**

The Waist Line

Let's think about this.

When you are separated or divorced, you are now put back into the dating scene, a scene where appearance is important. While going through separation, people are stressed. Stress causes most people to eat. When you are stressed, and eating, most of us tend to eat junk food and visit the fast food chains. These items tend to contain plenty of calories and head directly to your waistline or butt area. Appearance wise, this is not good. Being in your late thirties is bad enough, so having a pot belly or love handles just adds to the list of things women aren't looking for in a man. I see that the want list for a woman includes a full head of hair, money, a job, fit body, and a secure future. Hair, job and secure future I have, but the fit body is going to be a lot of work. It is so easy to browse through the candy machine at work, and on the drive home to an empty house, I much prefer a quick Big Extra meal versus having to make something by myself. How cruel is life when it comes to this. The one time you have to be at the top of your game, you end up not getting enough sleep, start to lose your hair, and eat way too much of unhealthy food. At the other end of the spectrum are the people who get so stressed that they don't eat at all, and resort to smoking, drinking and gambling. Now, in addition to not looking good, they smell and have no money. Here is where the diet fads come into play. Atkins, diet pills and weight loss clinics are prospering at an alarming rate. I would guess that if you polled the members of the clinics and the pill takers; that most of them are either already separated and starting a new life or they are planning to leave their spouse, but want to get a head start on the search for a new companion.

Once again, the fashion/personal appearance industry makes a killing from others hardships. Fitness facilities and cosmetic surgery businesses use the slogan of building a new you, which basically says "You best change your appearance, because you can't succeed with what you have". I believe that you need to start feeling good about yourself inside before you can work on the exterior. You have to love yourself and appreciate your own body before you have a chance of letting someone into your heart. Compliments from others will blow right by if you don't have a positive self attitude. Children love their parents regardless of their appearance or body composition. They love because of the love and compassion inside. Unfortunately, in the dating world without a good appearance people don't spend the time to find out what's inside. Many a hidden treasure goes unfound because of this. Oh well, their loss.

The Marathon

Playing sports is what I love to do. I have been doing it for as long as I can remember. Hockey, golf, baseball and even lacrosse were my way of exercising and having fun. About four years ago, a co-worker and good friend agreed to help me reach my goal of learning to run. Run a marathon that is, since I already knew the basic mechanics of putting one foot in front of the other in a hurried pace. Steve was an excellent guide and he had the patience required to get this hefty boy into marathon shape. We started with 20 minute runs and worked our way up to the 4-1/2 hours required to complete the 26.2 mile course. I started in the late summer, when the mornings were comfortably cool, and through Steve's persistence I endured the sub zero mornings of winter. Balance is a skill that is sometimes forgotten, until you find yourself rounding a corner on an ice glazed sidewalk at 6:30am. I think the big reason I tried running was because it was something new to me and it became a challenge. That and the fact that Steve informed me that training like this allowed me to eat basically whatever I wanted and weight gain would not become an issue. Eat and not get fat? That was music to my ears, and it was the carrot that needed to be in front of me. After building up the required endurance, we moved to speed training and hill climbs. This I was told would allow me to finish the marathon in a comfortable yet quicker pace. The training was very basic and Steve had only a few rules or guidelines to follow. "Walk when you can walk and rest when you can rest." "Always run past the finish line and when it comes to race day, do not change your routine, no matter what advice fellow runners offer." Neither Steve nor myself realized it at the time, but the training and actual race has helped immensely in my overcoming the turbulence I now face. Runners in a race are mirror images of us in the marriage cycle. We come in all shapes, sizes and ethnic backgrounds. We all have different styles, and the most successful racers are the ones who are able to adapt to the surroundings, and who are in sync with their own individual style. In a marathon, all runners hit what is referred to as "the wall" late in the race. It is a point where your body starts to react to all the pounding and stress being forced on it. Your legs start to burn; your breathing starts to labor and you are ready to give up. There is no apparent relief in sight and others are passing by. The weak give in and stop, giving up on their end goal only to become bitter when they realize what they gave up. The winners are the ones who push through the pain, the moments of doubt and force themselves to the end. They realize that whatever pain they feel now will be more than offset by the feelings experienced as they cross the finish line. Through the separation, I have forced myself through the moments of pain. I have blanked out the thoughts of self doubt, as well as ignored the variety of ill directed advice from fellow divorcees. I have lived my life and loved my boys the same way I always have and will continue to do so. I will push my heart and soul to make myself reach the finish line, for I know that whatever pain I feel now, will be offset by my sons one day saying "Thanks Dad for doing what you did. We love you."

Advice

"But I'm good on my own. Thanks! I don't depend on anyone and I can't be disappointed! While never experiencing love, it sure beats the alternative of being hurt by someone"

These are words from someone who I really care about. She believes that if you don't put yourself out on a limb, then you can't get hurt. Despite the pain, hardship and mental anguish that I am enduring now, I would never have given up the 15 years of happiness that came before. In the song "The Dance", Garth Brooks sang "Yes my life is better left to chance. I could have missed the pain but I'd of had to miss the dance." My life has had so many great memories and moments that will never happen again. The dance at my wedding, the memories of my honeymoon, and the signing of our first mortgage will never be replaced. Battling sickness and death together, and experiencing the births of my children would have never occurred if I had decided to stay alone. Stay alone and save myself from heartbreak! Everything we do in our lives, from the moment we open our eyes, comes with a risk. There are far too many outside influences in society for us to be prepared for everything. SARS, drunk drivers, criminals and natural disasters can all impact our lives. Everyday we wake up could be our last and no one knows when it is going to be their day. Memories are what create our lives, and we grow for tomorrow by learning what we did yesterday. When I reflect on my life, the majority of memories are of happy times and exciting events. I remember at age five, when my parents purchased a gas station and restaurant just outside of Peterborough. I remember at age fifteen when I kissed Karen outside of the Lakehead Barn Dance. I remember standing in a parking lot outside of Port Hope shaking hands with my father. I was nineteen and heading off for my first year of college. These are moments that I remember vividly and it is because they meant something to me and involved people I cared about. I don't remember the nights I was sent to my room or spanked (maybe I was such a good kid, that it didn't happen), and I don't recall family pets dying. I do remember however all the fun I had with those pets. There was Shep, Marcie, Scout, and of late Chimo. The happy times definitely outweigh and overpower the sad times. If anyone who reads this book is single, and prefers to stay that way for fear of getting hurt, I have to tell you that I believe you are wrong. While people can be spiteful, revengeful and even murderess, the feelings you gain from being loved can never be destroyed. Open your heart and let someone in, or better yet try and love someone unconditionally and watch what happens. Being nice and loving towards another human being can never be a bad thing. Imagine if the whole world took this approach?

Childbirth

There is a club, that I am lucky enough to be a member of. It is the Parent Club and the rewards are endless. I remember during the pregnancy, how everyone informed me how having a son or daughter would alter my life. I kept asking what it is like watching the birth and even got hooked into the "Life Network" channel watching the many versions of childbirth. My brothers and friends all informed me that there were no words to describe the moment. They were right. Watching your first child, and for me the second as well, being born is unbelievable. It is something that can't be captured on video or put down in books. No matter how hard you try, you can never explain to someone what it is like, if they have not gone through it. At my work it is very common to have a fellow employee going through the new parenting stage, and it is so much fun to be able to compare our stories. Some cannot understand how a woman can put her body through such a process. You discuss the labor time, the use of drugs if required and about those first few days at home with the new addition. It is something that we can only relate to if we have gone through it ourselves. If you haven't, then you just can't fathom the joy, happiness, and elation that comes along with the life altering occasion. Death is the same. Many of us wonder how people faced with dying are able to go on and live a somewhat normal life. How do you get up each day, knowing that you are about to leave the earth, never to come back? How do you put others ahead of you and not take on a attitude of self pity? Dying, like childbirth is a select club, and only those who go through it can understand everything you feel and experience. Separation is the club I am a member of now. I didn't ask to join, and surely if there was a way out, I would find it. People ask me how

I deal with the feelings of betrayal, the emotions of being hurt and how I deal with my life alone. It is simple. Until you experience it, there are no words that I can use to explain everything. Video or snapshots will do nothing. You will only understand the feelings, and ride the rollercoaster of emotions when you become a member. Trust me, this is one club you do not want to become a member of, and I hope you do everything in your power to be on the outside looking in. The grass is definitely not greener on this side.

The Next Step

There is no final chapter. There is no storybook ending. This is not a movie or reality series. There is no winner on the last page. The winners are the lawyers, and only the lawyers. Everybody else has lost something somewhere amongst all of this. My cat, which we got six months into our marriage, was buried today. I dug the hole with the help of my two boys. Alex helped fill the hole after Chimo was placed in. I felt that it was only fitting that I place my wedding ring into the gravesite as well. The cat, like my marriage had ended, and a burial is the final step in the process. A spruce cross colored by the two boys marks the gravesite and I am sure that the spot will never leave my memory. Actually, the final phase of my broken marriage is yet to take place. That is when the lawyers draw up the final agreement; my ex-wife and I split our belongings and move on. In my situation, I feel that the laws have allowed my ex to gain unfair financial power when the ink dries. Everyone who goes through divorce and separation will have a different outcome. Some will fair better than I, some will wish that they were as lucky as I am. Details at this time do not matter. What matters, is that my new life is about to begin. What matters to me are my boys. They are the ones who make me want to wake up in the morning. Greg asked me if having a mommy and daddy was the most special thing in the world. I told him that having two special boys as sons was the best thing in the world for me, and that as long as his mommy and daddy loved him, he was as lucky as lucky could be. Some people consider winning a lottery as being lucky. I believe

Every Other Weekend

that by having healthy children and being able to experience their unconditional love makes me the lucky one. I know that financially, I will be on the short end of the stick for a very long time, but this separation process has made me realize something. Money is not what life is about. I haven't had the opportunity to overspend with Greg and Alex. Dinner at Boston Pizza, swimming at the local Best Western hotel, go-karting, buying inexpensive toys at the local Walmart, and spending a few hours at the local kid's Fun Stop has pretty much been the extent of my spending. But it hasn't hurt me. Most of our time together has been at the house. Going for bike rides to the park, running around the block, racing to the stop sign and back or playing hockey in the driveway has been the core of our excitement. We might watch a movie together, something like the Mighty Ducks…1, 2 and 3 of course or we might just watch Treehouse TV on a Sunday morning. These things have minimal monetary costs involved; however the joy and experience they yield are worth millions. I would pass up a day at Canada's Wonderland, or a weekend on a boat just to see the look in the boys' eyes as they try to chase me down in a game of sharks in the backyard. A twenty-minute walk through the neighborhood while having two little hands hold onto mine can never be packaged and sold in a store. These are cherished moments and occasions that are deposited right into my memory bank. They will be called upon during those cold winter nights, and I guarantee you that there is nothing money can buy that will ever replace them. No matter what comes through on the separation agreement, I know that I will survive. I might end up bankrupt, single and living in a cheap one bedroom apartment, but I will have something that no one can ever take away from me; the love from Gregory and Alex. Alex talks about needing my hugs and kisses and he calls it "needing Daddy time." Let me tell the whole world one thing. The boys will always have their "Daddy Time." No matter what! Even if it is Every Other Weekend!!!!

"There is no right reason to do something wrong"

Every Other Weekend

Conclusion

This book was never a plan in my life. Neither was separation, nor having to be forced away from my wife and boys. This book, I believe will be successful and so too will my future. There will always be second guessing and regrets about what has transpired, but hopefully everyone will move one. I was never exposed to broken marriages before, and I feel that if I was, then the process might have been smoother. What I have gone through is something that I would not even wish on my worst enemy. Not even on the man that is now with my ex-wife! My only hope is that I might one day, by way of this book; convince at least one family to go the extra mile. If I can do that, then what I have endured will be worth it. A very good friend of mine, John, asked me "What has been the hardest part through all of this?" I will no doubt find someone in the future, and my ex will be just another acquaintance. My child support payments will eventually disappear and for now, they will be just another bill at the end of the month. The pain will be replaced by a new love and some new walls will become my home. The hardest part of all of this is what it has done to my boys. They, Greg and Alex love both their parents equally and want to spend all their time with both of us. In reality, they can't and that is the pain that will never go away. Having your children say that want mommy and daddy together and you can't deliver, hits deeper than anything that I can imagine. A tear will always form because of this. That pain will never end. There is no conclusion to this book. Everything that happens from here on out will be as a result of the previous. Maybe, ten years from now, I will write a new book and see where the good Lord has taken me. The real conclusion will be when I have passed on. The future roads that my children travel will reflect the teachings that hopefully they have absorbed from me. As you turn this final page, please remember the following: "In sickness and in health: for better and for worse; in good times and in bad, until death do we part"

"When it comes to a relationship, it is far better to sit together with a counselor, than it is to sit alone with a divorce lawyer."

Afterthought

Before sending this book to publishing, I had some people read it, so that I could get an idea on if the book would sell or not. Everybody came back saying that the book was easy to read and it gave them insight as to what I was faced with. A common statement was that the book didn't have a happy ending or show hope at the end. The picture of the traffic light was to indicate that we all must move on and start again. It does not mean that all is forgiven or that everything is rosy. I am not happy about my situation and while I may move on, I will never stop wanting what I had. I still believe that I should have had one marriage and one family. I still believe that my boys should be able to be with both parents everyday. I still believe that the house in Wyevale should be the home for me and my family. This is not a movie, and while the world continues on, I, like many others will never fully escape the pain and hurt from a lost love. The peaks and valleys of happiness and sorrow will end up being a bearable existence of neutral ness. An amputee will move on in life after losing a limb. They learn to adapt with what they have. The fact is though, they always think about what could have been and what they are missing. I am the same. Don't think that life will be better because of what happens. It will be different, but it will never be better than what we initially plan for in life. Those who survive are those who can put the memories behind them. That is something I am not good at. I will always wish I had what was taken away. Always!

Towanda

I mentioned in my opening pages about Towanda. She is the one who loves me for who I am. Who is Towanda? She is my soul mate. She is my life mate. She is tall, yet at the same time she can be at the level of my youngest and be a part of his world. She is sophisticated as an artist, yet she can be in a child's world at the smallest of urgings. Towanda stimulates my body and can also ease away all my concerns with a simple smile. Towanda is elegant in her actions, yet she can have a snowball fight with the best of them. There are children's books that talk about the legend of peaceful women who take care of all the little kids and are the owners of a fun home. She resides at a place where people of all ages know they can go to find solace and security. The legend speaks of hot chocolate, fun games and warm treats. It talks of music, dancing and puppet shows. Towanda is that legend. She is the woman that kids were made for. Blonde? Well to tell you the truth, Towanda can be whatever you want her to be; blonde, brunette, redhead, auburn. She can dress up for a night on the town, or she can be in overalls to help you paint. Wow you say!

Where do you find someone like that? Is she for real? Does Towanda really exist? Or, is she just a dream of mine. Is Towanda a far stretched wish in everyone's life? Is she just like the "pot of gold" at the end of the rainbow? Yes she is…kinda. She is definitely at the end of the rainbow. The end of my rainbow, and everyone knows that a rainbow appears after the storm has passed through. The past two years of darkness and conflict has been my storm. The lightning strikes were fast and furious and my tears were the rain. Torrential at times but now subsided. The rainbow has appeared and very soon my journey to the end of my rainbow will be complete. How will I know that I am the end? It is very simple. My "pot of gold" will be there. My Towanda will be there. Be patient Towanda, for I am so close to finding you.

Lightning Source UK Ltd.
Milton Keynes UK
UKHW012021270223
417748UK00002B/5/J